THE LITTLE BOOK OF
WALES
RUGBY

Independent and Unofficial

Edited by

GARY BAKER

CARLTON
BOOKS

Text and design copyright © Carlton Books Limited 2019

A CIP catalogue record for this book is available from the British Library.

ISBN 978-1-78739-238-0

Printed in Dubai

CONTENTS

INTRODUCTION

WALES has never been a nation of people who hold back their views on the sport that is close to a national obsession, and there is no doubt the rugby men and women of the principality have the gift of the gab.

Over the decades, the great, well-known and lesser-noted names have spoken words of wisdom, been involved in high-profile controversy or shared off-the-cuff remarks of wit and humour that have become the stuff of legend. When 1950s legend Ken Jones scored a try, it caused the father of fly-half Cliff Morgan, in his excitement, to lose his false teeth, never to be found. And there is the truth behind the legendary phrase spoken by Barry John to Gareth Edwards concerning "you throw the ball, I'll catch it".

The great Carwyn James on coaching, Grand Slam celebrations, British Lions comments and the words spoken by those at the centre of some of the nation's biggest scandals, political upheavals and highest profile fall-outs are here in *The Little Book of Wales Rugby*. Also glorious moments … What did Mike Ruddock say to Gavin Henson after he kicked THAT 45-metre penalty to beat England in Cardiff? Graham Henry, in his own words, on why he had to leave the Welsh coaching job, ref Nigel Owens' wit and humour in the middle of the toughest of Test matches, and the late, great Ray Gravell cracking a superb one-liner when late tackling a South African during a Lions tour.

Throughout its pages, *The Pocket Book of Wales Rugby* will stir up memories of great days, big controversies and the glorious humour that the nation's players and public have in their DNA.

Enjoy reading!

CHAPTER 1

LAND OF MY FATHERS

"After the game, supporters burst into the dressing-room and ripped the laces from our boots. By about 7pm, on my way to see Dad, who'd been too ill to be at Stradey, there were policemen cavorting with a ball! By 8.30, as Max Boyce says in his song about the game, all the pubs had run out of beer!"

Phil Bennett on Llanelli's famous 9–3 win over New Zealand at Stradey Park, 31 October 1972

"We had a great side. Think of the names: Derek Quinnell, Phil Bennett, Barry Llewellyn, Gareth Jenkins, Ray Gravell, JJ Williams. I remember telling them before we went out on the field that of all the honours I'd won in my career, I was willing to give them all away for that one game."

Delme Thomas, Llanelli captain, on that win over the All Blacks

"I put my hands up and hit it. I think I tripped over the line through the gap and then there was the ball and I just pounced on it. You don't realise you are part of history until years and years later."

Llanelli try-scorer **Roy Bergiers** recalls his charge-down of an All Blacks clearance kick and scoring in 1972

"Undoubtedly the strongest wing I have ever seen."

JPR Williams talks about Cardiff, Wales and British Lions legend John Bevan

"Behave yourself, son, and nothing will happen to this ear of yours."

Pontypool legend **Bobby Windsor** to Bath's Gareth Chilcott after locking his teeth around Chilcott's earlobe before letting go

"I drove my shoulder into a ruck and obviously someone didn't like it, their reaction was to grab me by the head and shove their finger in my eye. Obviously it hurt but as a hooker you get used to taking that sort of thing ... My vision was so blurred I virtually threw the next line-out to their scrum-half."

Garin Jenkins, Wales hooker, on having a finger poked in his eye during the 1999 World Cup match with Argentina

"I remember just seeing the reaction of the players on the pitch and then I saw the medics. I knew something was very wrong. I could see his whole body convulsing. He had turned purple and they had to intubate him. You can't ever forget a moment like that."

Kat Czekaj on her Welsh international husband Chris Czekaj when he was knocked out when playing for French side Colomiers

"He then clobbered me, catching me when I was vulnerable, coming out of a scrum and gasping for air with my jaw loose. I don't think he intended to do the damage he did; he just wanted to intimidate me, but he caught me with a heavy blow and I had to leave the field with my jaw in tatters."

Tight head prop **Graham Price** on having his jaw broken by a punch from Steve Finnane, Australia v Wales, 1978

"I heard about one second of noise and then it went deadly quiet for me for the rest of the match. Maybe it was concentration, but I didn't hear the crowd at all, even after I scored my try, The first thing I did back in the changing-room was to ask our physio Gerry Lewis for a fag."

Keith Jarrett, Wales full-back, recalls his incredible Wales debut when he scored 19 points against England in 1967

"There was a lot of internal bleeding going on but it was important to the team to stay on. I dared not leave the field because we would have had only 14 men until a replacement arrived and that might have been time enough for France to score."

Mervyn Davies continued playing during the 1976 Grand Slam victory over France in Cardiff with a hole in his shin after being studded

"It's emotional every time I sing the anthem. I wish she was there watching. She was a massive supporter. Like any mother, she used to go over the top and I had to rein her in a bit."

Wales and Dragons hooker **Elliott Dee** talks about his late mother

"I think we must have a licence for it. The strange thing is that it involves different personnel, yet it seems hereditary that at some stage we will shoot ourselves in the foot. Every time, you think it can't happen again. How do you explain it? It must be a Welsh characteristic."

Wales and Lions legend **John Dawes** after Mike Ruddock is sacked as Wales national coach

"Everybody knew Grav was a proud Scarlet. Of course, his 'West is Best' catchphrase has gone down in legend and is emblazoned across one of the stands at the new Parc Y Scarlets. People loved and respected him because he wanted everybody to do well – as long as you didn't beat his beloved Scarlets!"

British Lions, Wales and Llanelli fly-half **Stephen Jones** pays tribute to Ray Gravell

"In 1823, William Webb Ellis first picked up the ball in his arms and ran with it. And for the next 156 years, forwards have been trying to work out why."

Sir Tasker Watkins, former WRU president, whose statue stands outside the Principality Stadium in Cardiff

"No leadership, no ideas. Not even enough imagination to thump someone in the line-out when the ref wasn't looking."

Wales fullback **JPR Williams** on Wales losing 28–9 against Australia in 1984

"Don't ask me about emotions in the Welsh dressing room. I'm someone who cries when he watches Little House on the Prairie."

Wales second row **Bob Norster**

"I didn't know what was going on at the start in the swirling wind. The flags were all pointing in different directions and I thought the Irish had starched them just to fool us."

Mike Watkins, on playing for Wales at a blustery Lansdowne Road, Dublin in 1984

"Am I? Brilliant."

Wales captain **Colin Charvis** on being told he had
been voted Wales's third sexiest rugby player

"The sooner that little so-and-so goes to rugby league, the better it will be for us."

Former England three-quarter **Dickie Jeeps** hails new Welsh star Gareth Edwards in 1967

"I think you enjoy the game more if you don't know the rules. Anyway, you're on the same wavelength as the referees."

Jonathan Davies lays into the officials on A Question of Sport in 1995

"A couple of years ago, I struggled to use a keyboard and writing emails was a nightmare. Now I'm using a computer every day and have joined Twitter, which is great fun – though my kids think it's a bit embarrassing."

Llanelli and Wales No.8 **Scott Quinnell** on his battle with dyslexia

"To a small junior school kid, Mervyn Davies was even more of a giant, when stood next to you in the flesh, than his colossal reputation led you to imagine. It was 1975 and I could not believe that one of the most talked about players on the planet ... was standing in our kitchen."

Wales scrum-half **Robert Jones** on meeting his hero Mervyn Davies

CHAPTER 2

HEROES OF
THE SHIRT

"Having had enough of getting soaked, when Gareth asked how I wanted the ball thrown to me next, I just replied, 'Oh, you throw it and I'll catch it ... let's go home'."

'The King', **Barry John**, to half-back partner Gareth Edwards at a rain-soaked Welsh training session. It is his most famous quote

"You've got to get your first tackle in early, even if it's late."

Llanelli and Wales legend **Ray Gravell**

"It's the first time I've been cold for seven years. I was never cold playing rugby league."

Jonathan Davies, a dual code star, on returning to Wales to play union after a stint in rugby league

"Bloody typical, isn't it? The car's a write-off. The tanker's a write-off. But JPR comes out of it all in one piece."

Gareth Edwards, on how legendry full-back JPR Williams survived a car crash

"(Rugby) League is much more physical than Union, and that's before anyone starts breaking the rules."

Adrian Hadley a dual code winger in 1988

"You knew that if you threw it anywhere in his vicinity he would catch it. He was also a masterful tackler and able to wrap up the opposition with ease. Invariably he'd emerge from the bottom of any ruck, killing opposition ball and slowing the ball down to help the team."

Wales No.8 **Mervyn Davies** – Merv the Swerve – is remembered by his friend and Llanelli No.8 Derek Quinnell

"I honestly did not have any idea about this until they called out my name but this is not just about me, it is for all of those players from the golden team that I played with."

Sir Gareth Edwards CBE, after receiving the Welsh Sports Personality of the Year Lifetime Achievement award in 2015

"It was awesome. I loved every minute of it and the icing on the cake was to get the win as well."

Centre **Hadleigh Parkes** recalls his Wales debut in the 24-22 Autumn Test win over South Africa in 2017, only the second Wales victory against the Springboks

"If I had my time again I'd be a soccer manager, not coach of a rugby club where half a dozen or more committeemen interfere with selection. As well, money now permeates rugby's administration. Rugby must always be our aristocratic heritage, never a trade."

Carwyn James, legendary British Lions and Llanelli coach

"This new midfield 'crash-ball' is a disaster – hunks of manhood with madness in their eyes, battering-ram bulldozers happy to be picked off on the gain-line by just-as-large hunks from the opposing side. For what? Just to do it all over again."

James expounds on the crash ball

"We are breeding robots. Is it the drudge and monotony of training sessions where everything's done by numbers? Fly-halves even call moves before the scrummage forms – 'miss one', 'dummy scissors', 'high up-and-under' and so on – regardless of the quality of the emerging ball. Coaches treat players like puppets on a string."

Carwyn James, a true visionary

"We are entering a very different world. The game will change for all concerned, including players and administrators alike. The challenge is to retain the special character which has helped make rugby so popular. The decision of the council is an extremely positive and bold one."

Wales' **Vernon Pugh** announces that the "'amateur" game was "open", thus heralding the dawn of professionalism in 1995

"I don't want to be known as a gay rugby player. I am a rugby player first and foremost. I am a man. I just happen to be gay. It's irrelevant. What I choose to do when I close the door at home has nothing to do with what I have achieved in rugby."

Former Welsh captain **Gareth Thomas** comes out and announces he is gay

"I didn't think about it ... it was purely instinct. It was a slippery ball. I steadied myself and concentrated to make sure I gathered it. I saw three All Blacks coming towards me and just dropped a goal. They flattened me and I didn't see where the ball was going, but the roar told me that it went over."

Newport's **Dick Uzzell** on his drop goal that beat the All Blacks 3-0 in 1963

"All I can remember thinking is two things. Firstly how great it felt to get a try against South Africa, a team I was more used to suffering a beating against, and secondly that it was a great time to get the score, shortly before half-time."

Mark Taylor, on scoring the first ever try at the Millennium Stadium in 2000 when Wales beat South Africa 29-19

"I was on the ground and could hear the Neath pack thundering towards me. It seemed certain that I was going to be given a raking. From nowhere, Dai dived on top of me, saying: 'Stay down'. He took an absolute shoeing for me. That was Dai, someone who was always thinking about others. A great man."

Phil Bennett playing for Llanelli against the legendary Neath and Wales flanker Dai Morris at The Gnoll

"When Ken Jones scored our second try, dad was so excited that his dentures flew out of his mouth into the crowd and he hasn't seen them since."

Cliff Morgan recalls a 14–3 Welsh victory over Ireland when he was commentating for the BBC

"I was never coached by anybody, even when playing for Wales. That may be the case for most goal-kickers, because very few clubs, when I was developing, had specialist people. I had natural kicking ability and I was kicking in rugby from a very early age. I think all goalkickers get the yips. I've certainly had the yips."

Fullback **Paul Thorburn**, who kicked an international record 70-yard penalty against Scotland at the National Stadium, Cardiff, in 1986

"We've lost seven of our last eight matches. The only team that we've beaten was Western Samoa and it's a good job we didn't play the whole of Samoa."

Gareth Davies, as Wales' results nosedived following the 1987 World Cup – they lost to Western Samoa in the 1991 World Cup

"I'd lined up a kick when suddenly someone shouted: 'I'll have a pint he doesn't kick it'. Someone else shouted: 'I'll have a pint as well'. I looked at the crowd and said: 'I'll take two of you on and no more'. I was just about to take the kick when the referee said: 'I'll have a half as well!'"

Barry John, about to miss a conversion to win the game for Cardiff in a 1970s club match at Swansea

"We did not put that much pressure on ourselves. It was the character we showed against Australia, where we would have fallen away and lost the game, the great performance against Tonga and against South Africa. It was a very successful Autumn campaign."

Jonathan Davies, after Wales beat South Africa in November 2018 to win all four Autumn Tests for the first time

"He (Ellis Jenkins) did all the hard work, I just finished it off. It is not something I do very often. That is my first try for Exeter or for Wales."

Prop **Tomos Francis**, on scoring his first try for Wales in the November 2018 victory over South Africa, after a break from man of the match Ellis Jenkins

CHAPTER 3

SVENGALIS IN THE STANDS

"I'm going to coach Wales – and I'm leaving tonight."

Graham Henry tells the world press of his
appointment as Welsh national coach in 1998

"When I left Wales, I had to walk. The combination of that and the Lions tour was a huge challenge, a challenge before my time really, but you don't say 'no' to those things. I resigned from Welsh rugby and got out of there before I died there."

The "Great Redeemer" **Henry** on leaving the Welsh national coaching job in 2002

"It looked like a clear try. It was such a big decision in the game. You fly a guy over from New Zealand and he has one big call to make. I think he has made a terrible mistake. You could see on the replay that Anscombe got there first. He put his hand on the ball and grounded it."

Warren Gatland on Gareth Anscombe's disallowed try during Wales' 12-6 defeat against England at Twickenham in the 2018 Six Nations

"A lot of the Welsh public had not seen Wales win a Grand Slam or Triple Crown so I was incredibly pleased for those people. It was a fantastic day and a fantastic occasion and a sense of excitement."

Mike Ruddock, in 2005, after Wales beat Ireland 32-20 in Cardiff to take their first Grand Slam since 1978

"I'm very upset for Gareth. I felt he was the right man to stay there. Was there a period for reflection and go through the correct process to come up with a recommendation? The same people who employed him 18 months ago are the same people who turned up this morning to say they have made a mistake."

Lyn Jones blasts the WRU over the sacking of Gareth Jenkins as national coach

"Philippe Saint-Andre is not Bourgoin's manager any more. To read that he was in touch with the Welsh Rugby Union was the straw that broke the camel's back. He should have told me about it and he didn't."

French club **Bourgoin** sack Saint-Andre for applying to become the Wales national coach in 2004

"I am not vindictive. I'd like to thank the WRU for giving me the opportunity. If I wasn't good enough, I wasn't good enough. My only regret is not seeing my contract through to the World Cup. Looking back, I enjoyed the experience. I don't think I'd have changed anything."

Kevin Bowring, speaking in 1999 after his 29-Tests reign as national coach

"I have not the ability nor strength of character to bear the whole burden of the Welsh nation as a panacea for all ills."

Alan Davies, national coach, after Wales went out of the 1991 World Cup

"'Paul, it's Steve. I'm just ringing you to let you know that you haven't made the World Cup squad.' He went on to give me a load of compliments and told me to maintain my form, saying I was young and would come through. He made you feel good about yourself and it gave me a massive confidence boost."

Prop **Paul James** recalls kind words from national coach Steve Hansen in 2003

"I'm quite old fashioned and I have to say that if these players want to go to England to earn more money, they should realise it could jeopardize their selection for Wales. That is not a threat. It simply reflects the fact that if they're playing in England, it's harder for the coaching team to go to see them."

National team manager **Alan Phillips** supports Graham Henry's stance on players playing outside Wales in 2000

"New Zealand is just a poxy little island in the South Pacific."

Wales assistant coach **Scott Johnson**, before they played the All Blacks in autumn 2004

"I wasn't misquoted, I just got it wrong – it's actually two poxy islands."

Johnson tries to joke about his faux pas the day before the match

"The key thing to say is that no-one would deny the total commitment, passion and dedication that Gareth Jenkins has given to the cause. His desire for success has been tangible – you can taste it, you can smell it when you are in his company – but it was not to be."

WRU chief executive **Roger Lewis** praises national coach Gareth Jenkins despite sacking him following the 2007 World Cup exit

"We got the stadium built on time and within budget, have created long-term jobs in Wales and make a huge contribution to the Welsh economy, yet our local rates are five-fold what we paid at Cardiff Arms Park and we have to find around £5m a year to run the stadium."

Chairman **Glanmor Griffiths**, in 2001, slams the rocketing costs levied on Millennium Stadium PLC during the build of the arena

"I stand down with genuine optimism for the future of Welsh rugby. We've come to grips with professionalism. The board will ensure a more efficient, effective and streamlined professional administration. The new five regions were essential for our top flight club rugby to be both viable and competitive."

Glanmor Griffiths quits as Welsh Rugby Union and Millennium Stadium PLC chairman in 2003

"There is an expectation and a passion for rugby in this country which we have to meet. We are stewards of the game. We have to deliver for the people. It's as simple as that. I like to get things done, I like to get results and I like to move quite quickly."

David Moffett, on taking over as Welsh Rugby Union chief executive in 2002

"My reasons for leaving are personal and family and I don't have another job to go to, but we will be returning to live in New Zealand. In many respects it's a lot like Wales and we've loved every minute of living in Wales, but our families are down in that part of the world."

David Moffett resigns as WRU chief executive in 2005

"I think Tony is a bit lost in action here. He has only attended one meeting with the WRU and the regions over the last six years – and that was this year. So, I didn't quite know what to make of Tony's comments there because we have been working hard with the people who are at the sharp end of regional rugby."

WRU chief executive **Roger Lewis** responds to calls from Newport Gwent Dragons non-executive director Tony Brown about increased funding for the four regions in 2012

"I woke up this morning and my face – well, my tonsils – were everywhere. A couple of the girls texted me asking me to remember them when I am famous."

Fan **Lisa Jones**, caught on the Principality Stadium big screen belting out the Welsh national anthem before the win over Scotland in the Autumn 2018 Test

"That ref, mun, he has only got one eye."

One-eyed fan **Terry Morgan** disputes a call made by the referee during Wales's 2018 Autumn Test victory against Scotland

"Clive would pace the room, fag in hand, and demand you performed not just for yourself, but for your father, your mother, your long-lost aunt, the miners, the steelworkers, the teachers, the schoolchildren – in effect the whole Welsh nation. You were their representatives and you owed it to them to deliver."

Phil Bennett describing a Clive Rowlands motivational speech before a Wales international

"In all the times I have been to Cardiff for the rugby, I've seen some very drunk people but never any trouble."

Fan **Julia Roberts** reacts to the news of an alcohol-free zone being set-up at the Principality Stadium in 2018

CHAPTER 4

SIX NATIONS EPICS

"After the match, after we had beaten England and were back in the dressing room, Mike Ruddock, our coach, told me he couldn't watch. 'Why not? I knew I was going to kick it.' And it wasn't bravado. I did. I really did."

Gavin Henson, on his 45-metre penalty that saw Wales beat England at the Millennium Stadium 11-9

"It was an unbelievable atmosphere in the stadium, the support was tremendous. It would be difficult for any visiting team in Cardiff on a day like this, the fans carried us through."

Shane Williams on winning the 2005 Grand Slam

"It's just brilliant, a credit to the team, the squad and the management. Ireland played well to come back, but our gallant defence showed the squad's character. It's a first Grand Slam for 27 years, we're over the moon!"

Scrum-half **Dwayne Peel** after Wales beat Ireland 32–20 to win the 2005 Grand Slam

"After winning the Slam, people like Gavin and Shane Williams became superstars overnight. I wasn't in the limelight as much – maybe no-one knew who I was because of the scrum-cap, but I noticed how my value increased in the marketplace. I had offers from England and France but stayed at the Dragons for another year before moving to Harlequins."

Wales centre **Hal Luscombe** on his career after winning the 2005 Grand Slam

"He is good for the game and I am very happy that he said what he did because we are on a great run in the Six Nations. We are very pleased with that and we hope to continue it. Thank you very much Scott."

Shaun Edwards talks about Scotland coach Scott Johnson ahead of their 2013 Six Nations clash

"My priority as captain has been that performance has to come first; it is why you get picked. There have been a number of occasions since 2011 when I thought I needed to focus on playing well: you need to step back and look at yourself. There are times, even in a team sport, when you need to be selfish."

Sam Warburton after being relieved of the Wales captaincy in January 2017

"I've talked all along about people having dreams and what more can I take away from this. It's absolutely amazing. We've defended superbly and that's what's won us this championship. It's just been a magnificent eight weeks."

Captain **Ryan Jones** on the 2008 Grand Slam victory

"It's an unbelievable feeling. There's 30 or 40 people who have worked so hard for this. Everyone talks about their front five but ours were unbelievable throughout the tournament. The amount of unseen work they do is immense, and they allow the likes of the back row, Shane and the other backs to shine."

Flanker **Martyn Williams** on Wales' 29-12 win over France in 2008 that sealed their second Grand Slam in three years

"It was good to have dialogue with World Rugby over the weekend. They've confirmed the TMO made a mistake. That dialogue happens throughout international periods."

Rob Howley on the try that wasn't in Wales' defeat to England in 2018

"In Wales, you go from one extreme to another. I've had my ups and downs, but I'm certainly enjoying things at the moment. It's tremendous. I'm not just a winger who sits on his wing having a cup of tea until the ball comes my way. I'm hungry and I want to get involved as much as I can."

Shane Williams after Wales' 16-12 win in Dublin during the 2008 Grand Slam run

"It was definitely an ugly win. Sometimes you will take an ugly victory over the performance. We turned up today and it was all about winning. The performance was not the most important thing. We started off well but there were too many turnovers and mistakes."

Warren Gatland after Wales defeated France 14–13 in 2018

"Warren is looking for control from me, bossing the boys around a bit and being a leader on the field. That is what I will be aiming to do. I have had the chance of watching Stephen Jones from the bench and he has controlled matches. He has been in outstanding form and now it is down to me."

James Hook looks to make his mark at the 2009 Six Nations

"Save for the hangover from hell, it was a day and an experience which left me very happy and I thank Wales for it."

Wales defence coach **Shaun Edwards** reflects on his side's Six Nations triumph

"We've chatted about various things, from the on-field technical stuff to the captain's role in a group function. Sam has been great. I have encouraged him to be vocal and visible – essentially it is still his side. He is squad captain."

Co-captain **Ryan Jones** talks about his colleague Sam Warburton after Wales's 2013 victory in Paris

"It was a good way to start the tournament ... I'm fortunate enough to have played in this competition a few times and know how important the first game is in giving you something to build on. I said in the autumn we were changing the way we play but it doesn't happen overnight. It's starting to pay off now."

Centre **Scott Williams** after Wales beat Scotland 34-7 in 2018

"It was the most dramatic game of rugby I've experienced in my life."

Wales assistant coach **Shaun Edwards** after they beat Scotland 31-24 with a dramatic last-gasp Shane Williams try

"I am over the moon. You have to put your body on the line to win a Grand Slam. It's just awesome."

Man of the match **Dan Lydiate** celebrates Wales' 2012 Grand Slam after a 16-9 win over France

"This makes all the sacrifices worthwhile. You have to give credit to the French, they made it difficult. But we won and that's what counts."

Skipper **Sam Warburton** on winning the 2012 Grand Slam after beating France

"Moving forward, we have to be pleased with the way we responded (against Italy), but it doesn't make up for the disappointment of last week. After 40 minutes of poor rugby, we've still finished second. We like to look at the negative side of things, but let's look at the positives ahead of a pretty tough tour to New Zealand."

Fly-half **Dan Bigger** tries to be positive after Wales finish second in the 2018 Six Nations

"I'm very grateful that [Eddie Jones] flagged it up, if someone's unsure in professional sport, it's important we get clarity. My parents have done that [told me I'm out of order] for many years, and I'm married now so it's just like being at home."

Alun Wyn Jones takes a swipe at England boss Eddie Jones in 2018

"JPR stood with his fists raised, the crowd erupted and a few minutes later, Wales had their Grand Slam."

Rugby historian, author and journalist **Huw Richards** recalls the famous "shoulder-charge" tackle by JPR Williams in Wales' 1976 clash with France

"That try against France to win the Grand Slam was a special day. That put me on top of the Welsh try-scoring record, above Gareth Thomas, and my father won £50,000 with that try as well."

Wing **Shane Williams** reveals his father placed a bet early in his career, that he would become Wales' record try-scorer

CHAPTER 5

RUGBY WORLD CUP HEROICS

"It's pretty tough on Rhys because he's a tremendous player. The policy we believe is working and hopefully when we go into the autumn everybody has got clarity. If we leave the door even slightly open for people, sometimes we think we give them false hope. We're absolutely going to stick with the policy."

WRU chief executive **Martin Phillips** on Rhys Webb's non-involvement in the 2019 World Cup after his move to Toulon

"It can be the most brilliant thing in the world and the most desperate thing in the world to be a Welsh rugby player. I was devastated to be out of the World Cup. We have sweated and bled for each other and I was devastated that has suddenly come to an end. It hurts."

Gareth Thomas reflects on Wales's 38–34 loss to Fiji at the 2007 World Cup

"The board of the Welsh Rugby Union met last night and David (Moffett) and I met with Gareth this morning. A decision has been made, which Gareth has accepted, that he is no longer the national coach of Wales. Our World Cup journey came to an end yesterday. It is now about 2011 and that is what today was about."

WRU chief executive **Roger Lewis** on national coach Gareth Jenkins' sacking after Wales 2007 Rugby World Cup exit

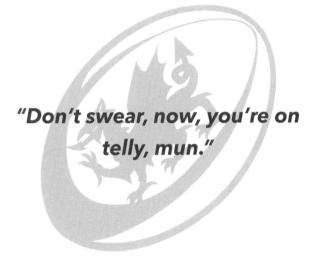

"Don't swear, now, you're on telly, mun."

Referee **Nigel Owens** warns New Zealand star Dan Carter about his language in 2015

"I went to mass this morning and even the priest came out and put his hands up in the air to celebrate."

Devout Catholic **Shaun Edwards** after Wales beat England in 2015

"In 1987, we reached the semi-finals of the inaugural World Cup and I believed we were in the process of developing into one of the world's top teams."

Wales scrum-half **Robert Jones**

"It is one of those games with mixed emotions. Scoring a try against the great All Blacks but having such a big score (against us) in the semi-final and the disappointment of losing – and remember there was only four points for a try in those days."

Centre **John Devereux**, who scored in the 49–6 defeat to New Zealand in the 1987 World Cup semi-final

"I had missed a couple during the game but was striking the ball well. Sometimes the margin between getting it over or not is very narrow. As soon as I struck it I knew it was over. It was great to see it go through the posts but we still had a couple of minutes to hang on."

Paul Thorburn on landing the winning kick in the third-place play-off against Australia in 1987

"In all honesty, playing the All Blacks in the semi-final was a daunting prospect. They were a superb team. We'd played Ireland and England and they weren't major obstacles. But playing the All Blacks was a very different story. They were so far ahead of us in the conditioning stakes that it was quite alarming."

Richard Moriarty reflects on playing the All Blacks in the 1987 semi-final and losing 49-6

"We had enough possession and territory. We paid the consequences. I still remember the boos ringing around the ground and there was total despair in our squad. The media was not good and quite rightly so. Up to that point it was probably the biggest shock in any World Cup and it was on our own doorstep."

Ieuan Evans on the shock 16-13 defeat to Western Samoa in 1991 in Cardiff

"If the players had bought into what Alex was trying to do we would have been successful in 1995. We had a very short space of time to train and for him to get his message across. The squad was probably Cardiff biased, and there was a lot of resentment from the other players, who didn't respond well to it."

Captain **Mike Hall** on Cardiff coach Alex Evans, who was brought in to coach Wales at the 1995 World Cup

"There is the real danger that the occasion will become bigger than the game. We're not a great team. Let's keep our feet on the ground."

National coach **Graham Henry**'s advice to the Welsh public before the 1999 tournament

"Whilst the nation's hopes and supporters' hopes were sky-high, there was a bit of reality with us. We knew we had the experience and we had to make that count. For whatever reason throughout that World Cup, we didn't have the consistency in our performance. I think we peaked before the World Cup started."

Rob Howley's bottom line on Wales' 1999 World Cup campaign

"We're very proud that we put in a very good performance and showed our character. But we still lost and it was one of those games that we could have played a little bit better, and had a better scoreline in the end. We knew we had to step up to perform against the New Zealanders and that's we did."

Wales skipper **Colin Charvis**, but it wasn't enough as they lost 53-37 in the pool stages to New Zealand

"We're gutted we couldn't get up but we've come a long way and I can't say any more than that. We came here to win it, we threw everything at them and they showed why they're a good side - they took that and in the end held on for the win."

Coach **Steve Hansen** on going out to eventual winners England in the 2003 tournament

"At half-time we knew that we were a better team than we had shown and we needed to prove that to ourselves and to other people. I think that we did that and emerged with an amount of credit. If Australia hadn't got the second try from [Chris] Latham it would have been game on."

Stephen Jones on losing 32-20 to Australia in the 2007 pool stages

"We just feel like the destiny of the result was taken out of our hands with the red card."

Warren Gatland, on Wales' heroic 9-8 defeat to France after Sam Warburton's dismissal in the 2011 World Cup semi-final

"We showed great character to come back. We were disappointed in the first-half performance, but we have a lot of respect for the Samoans. It was a big test in the scrums and lineouts. We knew we were going into the game in good physical shape and towards the end that started to tell."

Fly-half **Rhys Priestland** on Wales' 17-10 win over Samoa in the 2011 pool stages

"I don't think I've shown quite as much emotion in 80 minutes as I have today. This game was about this team wanting it badly enough and if you want that, it can happen for you. As a coach, the way they stuck at the task, I can't ask for any more. We wanted it more in the end."

Warren Gatland on Wales' 28-25 win over England in 2015

"People from outside might not think we have a strong squad but we have such resilience. Everyone trains hard, but we have been to some dark places in the summer and we didn't want that to go to waste. We have a difficult turnaround now. We will enjoy this for 24 hours but after that it is heads on."

Captain **Sam Warburton** gives his reaction to the win over England in 2015

"At the start the boys gave everything. They just weren't good enough to hang on in the last few minutes. I don't want to make any excuses. At the end of the day South Africa won the game. They hung in there right until the 80 minutes. They got one chance and they took it and that was the result."

Warren Gatland after Wales' 2015 defeat to South Africa

"There was nothing wrong with that tackle. If you want to dive like that again, come back here in two weeks and play, not today. Watch it."

Referee **Nigel Owens** rebukes Scotland's Stuart Hogg for "simulation" after a South African tackle at Newcastle's St. James' Park in 2015

CHAPTER 6

ROARING WITH THE LIONS

"I cannot praise my assistant Carwyn James too highly. From the day of our appointments, we began to think alike as far as the tour and its preparation was concerned."

Doug Smith, 1971 British and Irish Lions tour manager, lauds the single-minded dedication to the cause of coach Carwyn James

"James was an outstanding coach who did things in a simple, methodical way which made each member of the team realise that the player is an integral member of a great side. He was held in the greatest esteem by the team and the New Zealand officials."

Smith, continues his praise of James and his coaching ethos after he masterminded the historic defeat of New Zealand in 1971

"The Lions experience is a step ahead of home internationals. You have more wise men around you, no one is distracted from the game, you learn to play with judgement rather than pure emotion."

Sir Gareth Edwards talking about the 1971 tour to New Zealand

"He was frightened to death, and it takes a lot to frighten anybody who has been shouted at by Ray Prosser. 'Tom,' whimpered Bobby. 'I'm lost. I can't find my 'ut. Can I sleep with you?' Anybody who has spent much time jammed between Graham Price and Charlie Faulkner is used to living rough."

Welsh flanker **Tommy David** on compatriot hooker Bobby Windsor after a drinking session in South Africa on the 1974 tour

"I was skint so I went on a 15-week tour with £40 in my pocket. I had to do some ducking and diving while I was away, I can tell you."

Wales hooker **Bobby Windsor**, a steelworker, on the 1974 British and Irish Lions' undefeated tour of South Africa

"That's not something I'm proud of. Funnily enough, I bumped into him on a train from London to Cardiff years later and he asked, 'Do you remember me?' I had to admit that I didn't and he just said that he had played against me in South Africa in 1974. We had a lovely chat."

Full-back **JPR Williams** on his 60-yard run to deliver a right hook to Moaner van Heerden on the 1974 tour of South Africa

"We were pleased to have held the All Blacks in the First Test when our forwards showed their claws. What a pity the forwards did not play again with the same tigerish tenacity. It was if they had burnt themselves out in that one game."

Wales centre **Bleddyn Williams** on the 9-9 draw against New Zealand in 1950; the Lions then lost 8-0 and 6-3

"I found myself kissing my Lions jersey the other day as I was packing it up for another flight."

Sam Warburton treasures his first British and Irish Lions jersey on the tour of Australia in 2013

"I couldn't believe my luck or my eyes. Estimates as to how far I had to go to score that try vary. Resisting all temptation to stretch a point, I have to say that it was no less than six inches and no more than two feet."

Wales' wing **Ieuan Evans** on his match- and series-winning try against Australia in 1989 when David Campese made a horrendous error

"Of all the tries I scored for club and country the one that won the Third Test for the Lions against Australia in 1989 is clearly the most talked about. I have to say, though, that I remember all my tries: from schoolboy level to internationals. I just loved scoring; it was my job."

Evans, again, on that famous try that won the British Lions Test against Australia in 1989

"Let's pass this jersey now to the next generation in four years and we set this team in stone in Lions history forever."

Sam Warburton's inspirational captain's speech before the drawn final Test against New Zealand in 2017, leaving the series 1–1

"I have played enough professional and international level games to know what to expect tomorrow and if I felt for one second I wasn't going to be ready or good enough I would have told Rob Howley where to stick it."

Winger **Shane Williams** confident he would hold his own back in a Lions shirt against the Brumbies in 2013

"Looking back I feel horrendous for doing it now. I'll have to live with that and take it on the chin."

Wales winger **George North** apologises for his finger-pointing gesture at Will Genia during the Lions' 2013 Test defeat of Australia

"I had to put it behind me, but I also used the experience. I didn't want to feel like that again."

Full-back **Leigh Halfpenny** uses the disappointment of losing the second Test to Australia in 2013 as motivation for the decider

"The scoreline reflects what we wanted to do for the changing room which is not give up and represent our four countries with pride."

Wales lock **Alun-Wyn Jones**, who skippered the Lions to victory in the final Test against Australia in 2013

"Loftus (Versfeld) is the hardest place in the world to play rugby at this moment. Firstly, it's so because of the altitude, and secondly anybody who went there for the Super 14 final would have seen why it is the hardest place to play rugby."

Wales defence coach **Shaun Edwards** was part of the British and Irish Lions coaching team in South Africa in 2009

"Gethin Jenkins is one of the best loose-head props in the world. He hits up to 40 rucks a game, makes at least 10 carries and even more tackles. Those are amazing statistics for a prop and he is a very intelligent rugby player."

Warren Gatland, assistant British and Irish Lions coach in South Africa in 2009, talks about the Wales and Cardiff star

"He was a magical man to have in your team because he could turn a game with one run. Some of the tries he scored were breath-taking."

The 1971 British and Irish Lions captain **John Dawes** pays tribute to star wing Gerald Davies

"The tour party was made up of 29 players and a tour manager. There was nobody else - no coach, doctor, physiotherapist or pressmen. We could do as we liked without looking over our shoulders. We drank a bit and enjoyed female company, but we tended to carouse only after matches. Standards of behaviour were left to the individual."

Legendary Welsh British Lions star **Harry Bowcott** on the 1930 tour of New Zealand and Australia

"I was back in Cae Fardre; no noise, no distraction, no pressure. I took a few deep breaths and shook my arms as they hung straight down in front of me and I could hear the roar of the crowd as the ball went over. I could even hear a strain of 'Bread of Heaven'. And I was in heaven."

Fly-half **Neil Jenkins** recalls kicking for the Lions on the 1997 tour of South Africa

CHAPTER 7

CELEBRITY FANS

"Rugby is a wonderful show – dance, opera and, suddenly, the blood of a killing."

Richard Burton, Welsh actor

"Adam plays rugby with fire in his belly, steel in his spine and that mad mop of hair on his head. Anyone in public life with hair like that gets my vote, especially when they put their neck on the line and pull out all the stops for their colleagues."

Politician **Boris Johnson** hails Adam Jones, one half of Wales' "Hair Bear Bunch"

"I haven't felt like this since my uncle's funeral in 1986. We were in the cemetery when somebody got the score from the Arms Park – Wales 15, France 23. It cast a gloom over the whole proceedings."

Comedian and folk singer **Max Boyce**

"I know cos I was there!"

Max Boyce's words in his famous poem recalling
Llanelli beating the touring All Blacks 9–3 in 1972

"What unbelievable character! Mighty. Costly. Unforgettable. So proud!"

Actor **Michael Sheen** on Wales' World Cup victory over England

"On the school playing field I stayed as far away from the ball as possible, terrified of the studs on the boots of the other players who were bigger than me. It's only in the last 10 years that I've developed a love of the game. An ideal Saturday afternoon is now spent on the sofa watching the Six Nations."

Welsh comedian **Rob Brydon** in 2012

"One of the modern greats of rugby. Good luck for everything in the future."

Real Madrid football star **Gareth Bale** tweets his old Whitchurch School friend Sam Warburton on his retirement from rugby

Duke of Cambridge: *"You got a bit lucky at the weekend, didn't you?"*

Mako Vunipola: *"Yeah, yeah, we did,"* obviously not believing him.

Mako and **Billy Vunipola** meet the Patron of the WRU after beating Wales in the 2018 Six Nations

"I love to hear it being sung at Wales games. It makes me very proud to be Welsh, that they're using one of my songs to sing. That's important to me."

Sir Tom Jones on the unofficial Welsh anthem, his song "Delilah"

"Brave beyond belief. Better than winning four Brit awards. Million times better than headlining Glastonbury."

The Manic Street Preachers hit Twitter after Wales' World Cup win over England in 2015

"Ryan Giggs walked into the dressing room straight after the game at Twickenham. It was a real boost because there was some despair after losing to England. I was shell-shocked to get the chance to talk to Giggs. He's an absolute legend of Welsh sport."

Centre **Jamie Roberts**, on meeting football star and future Welsh manager Ryan Giggs after defeat by England in 2014

"Just want to wish the Welsh team good luck pob lwc Cymru."

American actor **David Hasselhoff**, whose wife Hayley is from Glyneath, wishes the national team well

"Put it this way, I can't ever remember the rugby not being on. Growing up in Cardiff and then Swansea, it was just a fundamental part of my upbringing; those games would always be big events which pulled us all together."

Cerys Matthews, lead singer of Catatonia

"I grew up among heroes who went down the pit, who played rugby, told stories, sang songs of war."

Richard Burton

"The team probably weren't aware of the positive effect their success was having on the nation. I'm sure the hard work nurturing new talent from all corners of Wales will bear fruit. We saw it in the Rugby World Cup, with Sam Warburton, George North and Rhys Priestland, how young people can achieve great things with dedication and hard work."

Rosemary Butler, former Welsh Assembly Presiding Officer, in 2011

"As a boy I'd have done anything to play rugby union for Wales. I was a scrum half, and had a trial for Sale. My friend Danny said he heard me in training shouting, 'No, not the face!' and I realised it was time to move on. Cauliflower ears and a flat nose aren't good looks for a TV presenter."

Former *Blue Peter* presenter **Gethin Jones**

"A trouble-free train journey from London to Cardiff. A good seat at the world's best rugby stadium. An exciting game. A win for us. An evening's celebration with old friends. A leisurely trip back the following morning."

BBC news-reader **Huw Edwards** describes his perfect Welsh rugby day

"I'm trying to get hold of his (a friend's) mum to ask 'What ticket numbers are yours?' so then I can contact the Welsh Rugby Union and say I've got the tickets next to them and I can't get hold of his mum. Carol isn't answering the phone."

Comedian **Rhod Gilbert** on leaving his match tickets in London for a game in Cardiff

"His bike was like a garden gate. It was massive. He was so slow, I thought about checking my emails (on my phone)."

2018 Tour de France winner **Geraint Thomas** on a day spent cycling with Wales wing George North

"The stadium is a key component of what Wales has to offer as a host of major events. The stadium has set its sights on attracting high profile events of global importance which have attracted more visitors from outside Wales."

Carwyn Jones, First Minister of Wales, sings the praises of the Principality (then the Millennium) Stadium in 2013

CHAPTER 8

GOING INTO OVERTIME

"I have to praise Gareth for his quality kicks out of hand and obviously the winning kick from the touchline in front of that crowd in a European final. I just think it is phenomenal and shows the quality of player that he is."

Outgoing Cardiff Blues head coach **Danny Wilson** on Gareth Anscombe after his match-winning touchline penalty against Gloucester in 2018

"The boys are playing with smiles on their faces. It's a style that is not too dissimilar to how we play in New Zealand. Stephen (Jones) went there last year and chatted to the All Blacks about what they do and how they do it. We've implemented some of those things. Next year, they'll be looking to knock us off."

Scarlets head coach **Wayne Pivac** explains how they have adopted some New Zealand tricks after winning the 2017 Pro12 title

"From where we've come four years ago to now, we are at the top table of Europe and in the league. People asked whether last year was a fluke but we've shown it wasn't. We've improved in Europe and got to the semi. As long as we keep pushing ourselves, we will be alright."

Scarlets captain **Ken Owens** stays positive after losing the Pro14 title 40–32 to Leinster in May 2018

"I have read and heard a lot of nonsense that this is an asset-stripping property deal. Our vision is based on four regional entities to compete, successfully I hope, in competitions and to supply players for the national team. Retaining the four sides is important to allow opportunities for young players coming through. We need the Gwent people's support."

Welsh Rugby Union chairman **Gareth Davies** after the governing body took over the Dragons in 2017

"There was an incident with a lion, but, in fairness, it was nothing to do with the lion. He did bite Scott but when you put your hand in a fence where there is a lion, then you will get bitten. What TV wildlife show is there where you can pat a lion on the head like it's a kitten?"

Ospreys head coach **Steve Tandy** after hooker Scott Baldwin, visiting Bloemfontein Zoo in September 2017, was bitten by a lion

"I love playing for Northampton Saints and am excited by the potential of the squad that is being assembled but, as a proud Welshman, I felt that now is the right time to move back home despite the compelling offer Saints made me."

Wales wing **George North** leaves Northampton for the Ospreys amid a spat with the Saints in March 2018

"I will be open about the things that need to improve. I won't gloss over things, that's not my style as an entrepreneur. It's important to face challenges, talk about them and then agree what we are going to do about it. I have one thing underpinning it – I want the Dragons to be the best they can be."

Welsh millionaire and entrepreneur **David Buttress** on taking a stake and becoming Dragons chairman

"I didn't know the full implications when I agreed to join Toulon because the change in the selection policy came out after I signed. I have given 10 years' service to the Ospreys and Welsh rugby and have picked up injuries along the way. I would have hoped that would have been taken into consideration."

Ospreys and Wales scrum-half **Rhys Webb** is excluded from the national team because he joined Toulon before winning 60 caps

"The WRU is awaiting final confirmation from Celtic Warriors regarding the proposed buy-out of Pontypridd's 50% stake in their regional structure by Leighton Samuel. It is envisaged that a meeting between Mr Samuel and the WRU will take place early next week."

Welsh Rugby Union 2003 statement about a buyout by Celtic Warriors chairman Leighton Samuel of Pontypridd's shares in the region

"The last 10 years have been a tremendous time for me personally and professionally, both at Neath RFC and, subsequently, at the Ospreys. We've come a very long way since the summer of 2003 when Neath and Swansea came together to form the Ospreys, and I take great satisfaction in our many achievements over the past five years."

Coach **Lyn Jones** on leaving the Ospreys for pastures new in 2008

"What should never be forgotten is that livelihoods are at stake. There's a huge amount resting on the next couple of weeks. Not just players and coaches are involved in this regional game, there are support staff all interested in the outcome. Supporters have put their hands in their pockets time and again and it's important everyone resolves matters."

Scarlets coach **Simon Easterby** during a power struggle between the four regions and the WRU in 2013

"The job of Welsh coach is like a minor part in a Quentin Tarantino film: you stagger on, you hallucinate, nobody seems to understand a word you say, you throw up, you get shot. Poor old Kevin Bowring has come up through the coaching structure so he knows what it takes ... 15 more players than Wales have at present."

Mark Reason on the perils of coaching the national team in Wales in 1996

"I wanted a play that would paint the full face of sensuality, rebellion and revivalism. In South Wales these three phenomena have played second fiddle only to the Rugby Union which is a distillation of all three."

Playwright **Gwyn Thomas** in the introduction to his popular 1963 play *Jackie The Jumper*

"The relationship between the Welsh and the English is based on trust and understanding. They don't trust us and we don't understand them."

RFU secretary **Dudley Wood** on the state of Anglo-Welsh rugby relations in 1986

"They defend a lead like my mum pole vaults."

Commentator **Gwyn Jones** lays into the Scarlets in 2008 after they led Harlequins 19–3 at the break, but lost 29-22

"Wales! Who knows Wales? It's this little **** place that has got three million people – three million!"

England's **Eddie Jones** causes fury in Wales after his comments when speaking at a company conference

"We've had a talk about the problems, but there's enough talk now and I want to see action. We lost it up front and failed to control the set piece. They went for it all day and controlled the game."

Coach **Steve Hansen**, after losing 30-22 to Italy in Rome in 2003, their first defeat against the *Azzurri*

"There's no point in drawing inspiration from the past. We have to live in the here and now."

Wales defence coach **Shaun Edwards**

"There's no better feeling than sitting on the team bus travelling to the Millennium Stadium knowing that the team will be playing in front of 74,500 people. You're driven through the crowds where you see the smiles on people's faces and I get a huge buzz out of that."

Warren Gatland

"Playing against England does something to you. I could play against England today and do well. Welsh supporters, without a shadow of a doubt, are the best supporters in the world."

Clive "Top Cat" Rowlands, 1971 Wales Grand Slam coach and British Lions tour manager

"Mae hen wlad fy nhadau yn annwyl i mi, Gwlad beirdd a chantorion, enwogion o fri; Ei gwrol ryfelwyr, gwladgarwyr tra mad, Dros ryddid collasant eu gwaed."

"Gwlad, gwlad, pleidiol wyf i'm gwlad. Tra môr yn fur i'r bur hoff bau, O bydded i'r hen iaith barhau."

The **Welsh rugby public** singing the National Anthem at the Principality Stadium